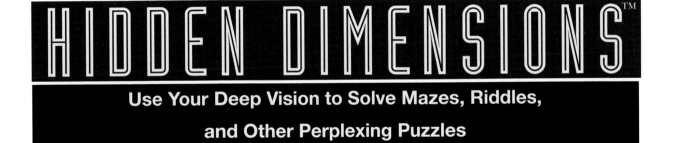

# HIDDEN DIMENSIONS™

## Use Your Deep Vision to Solve Mazes, Riddles, and Other Perplexing Puzzles

# DAN DYCKMAN

Harmony Books • New York

*For my brother Howard*

Published by Harmony Books, a division of Crown Publishers, Inc., 201 East 50th Street, New York, New York 10022. Member of the Crown Publishing Group.

Random House, Inc. New York, Toronto, London, Sydney, Auckland

HARMONY and colophon are trademarks of Crown Publishers, Inc.

Manufactured in the United States of America

Design by Lenny Henderson

Library of Congress Cataloging-in-Publication Data

Dyckman, Dan.

Hidden dimensions: use your deep vision to solve puzzles, mazes, and other perplexing puzzles / Dan Dyckman. — 1st ed.

p.   cm.

1. Puzzles.  2. Stereoscopic views.  I. Title.

GV1501.D93   1994

793.73—dc20

94-18286

CIP

ISBN 0-517-59994-5

10 9 8 7 6 5 4 3 2 1

First Edition

# CONTENTS

# INTRODUCTION

These Hidden Dimensions™ images are many things rolled up into one. They are made using a recently invented scientific principle for representing a three-dimensional image on a two-dimensional page. But they're not mere science. Since 1989, I've been working at bringing these images into the realm of art. I began working with simple black-and-white designs of random dots, portraying simple flat squares and rectangles, and I've consistently been pushing the forefront of the field, producing curved and rounded depth designs, adding colored, swirled patterns—and in this book you'll see some hints of even newer innovations.

But over the years, I've come to realize that simply making these fascinating artistic designs isn't enough. I want to tickle your fancy in every way possible, so I've created a variety of puzzles and brain teasers, ranging from easy to very difficult, that are guaranteed to keep you busy for quite some time. Many of these are completely new *types* of puzzles, invented specifically to take advantage of the unique three-dimensional nature of this new art form. You won't be able to find puzzles like these anywhere else, because they need that extra dimension of depth that can come only from these Hidden Dimensions pictures.

You'll also find a few familiar puzzles—such as mazes—that I've transformed into this depth-defying new format. When you follow the paths of the maze up and over, you won't be looking at just a flat picture. It will be as real as a sculpture standing in front of you, with paths weaving in and around each other.

Then, as a dessert, I've included an appendix that shows you some of my most exciting innovations. And—oh, yes!—there's even a section explaining how you might go about creating your own three-dimensional pictures.

You've never seen the likes of this book before. So get ready for a most unusual journey through the multiple dimensions of art, science, and (most of all) entertainment!

# HOW TO STEREOVIEW

Learning to stereoview these images is a gradual process. It may require several attempts and some patience at first, but don't get discouraged—it gets easier with each new success, as you learn exactly how it works.

The idea of stereoviewing these images is that you will be looking *through* the images. Think of how your eyes relax when you're staring blankly at a wall; you're not really looking directly at the wall, you're looking somewhere off into space . . . at something *beyond* the wall. The same principle applies to these pictures. You don't want to look directly *at the surface* of the page, but rather to gaze *through the page.*

Here are two methods to help you along.

## METHOD 1

After years of experimenting with different methods, I discovered one that seems to work the best for newcomers. Hold the Hidden Dimensions picture upright in front of you. Bring the picture close to your face, so that it is almost touching your nose. Allow your vision to relax—you will find yourself looking through the page. That's your starting point.

Now, gradually move the image away until it is about eight inches in front of your face. Try to keep your vision relaxed, as if you are staring through the page. If you can keep your gaze relaxed, you should soon be able to see a true three-dimensional image coming off the page. If you think about what you are doing, you'll realize why it may be so difficult to learn. Perhaps for the first time in your life, you must train your eyes to look *through* a page, yet focus *on* it. To get over this hurdle, you may want to keep your vision as unfocused as possible—don't worry, you will still see the three-dimensional image, even if your vision is so relaxed that the image is a bit blurry!

If you are having difficulty, keep in mind that the key word is *relax*. If you find your focus shifting and your vision jumps onto the page, relax and begin again. If you find yourself straining your eyes even the slightest bit, or peering intently as if you must cross your eyes, you are doing it wrong! Keep your vision slightly blurred, and pretend you are staring blankly.

People who try this method often say, "I get to the point where I can see some vague shapes, but as soon as I try to bring them into focus, my vision jumps so I'm looking directly at the page, and I'm not looking through the page anymore." If you find this happening to you, you're almost there! Keep your vision blurred and relaxed as long as you can. The first time you see the hidden depths in one of these pictures, you may see only a small hint of depth. Stay relaxed, and you will see the depths develop gradually.

## METHOD 2

This method uses the two marks you'll find accompanying each image. Although this method generally isn't as successful as the previous one, you may prefer it because it provides an indicator of how close you are to success. The illustration above shows what you will be seeing as you follow this method.

Hold a Hidden Dimensions picture about eight inches in front of you. Notice that the picture has two black marks above it; these are called *fusion dots*. Blur your vision until you can get each fusion dot to split into two. You might find that blinking one eye helps you to achieve this split.

Now comes the interesting part. Try to relax your vision so that you *increase the split.* Newcomers often find themselves "trying hard" to make the split increase, but it works only if you relax and let it happen.

When you increase the split enough, you'll find that the two middle ghostlike marks will overlap and fuse together to make a single mark. You may even notice a 3-D effect within the mark. Now, if you can gently look down into the image, you should see the Hidden Dimensions picture in all its glory!

You may find that you can get the black marks to split, but you can't widen the gap between them, or perhaps you can't quite get the two "middle" dots to merge. Don't fret! Get as close as you can, and then be patient. Our eyes have a special built-in ability to bridge that final gap, so you may see the two marks suddenly "snap" together automatically.

Once you've properly merged the two marks, you may notice that they have a small 3-D effect. This is a clue that you're doing it properly. Now, without breaking your gaze, try to look down smoothly into the multicolor image. There, you should see a solid shape popping off the page toward you!

If you happen to see a reverse image—meaning you see an image scooped out of the page—then you are actually doing the reverse method. Your eyes are crossing, rather than relaxing and looking through the page.

### Important Notes

If you normally wear glasses or contact lenses, you should keep them on when looking at these images.

A very small proportion of people—about 2 percent of the population—lack the ability to see depth altogether. If you lack the ability to see depth, you won't be able to see Hidden Dimensions pictures. But don't assume you lack depth perception just because you can't

stereoview! About 30 percent of all people have a difficult time seeing these depths, yet they have perfectly good depth perception.

Stereoviewing as described in these methods can improve your eye control and strengthen eye muscles—in fact, it resembles certain eye exercises that opthalmologists may prescribe to correct mildly crossed eyes. However, if you have a medical condition known as wandering eye or lazy eye, meaning that one eye is turned inward or outward, or a history of strabismus, then you should consult your ophthalmologist. If you find yourself straining your eyes, or if your eyes feel tired and ache, or if the area around your eyes aches, you should stop what you are doing and try again another time. Stereoviewing these images properly should be a relaxing experience.

# HOW DOES 3-D WORK?

In order to understand how Hidden Dimensions pictures work, it may be helpful to understand how 3-D works in general.

We see depth because our eyes are spaced a few inches apart. Our left eye sees the world from a slightly different vantage point than our right eye, and our mind compares what our left eye sees with what our right eye sees; it identifies the slight discrepancies between the two perspectives and interprets them as depth cues.

For an example of this, hold a finger up in front of you while looking at some other object far away, like a picture on the wall. Now, still looking at the picture, alternate blinking your left eye and your right eye. Do you notice how your finger jumps from side to side? Because your finger is *closer* to you than the picture, it *shifts more* when you look at it with your left eye and then with your right eye.

Three-dimensional images operate by creating two pictures that mimic these discrepancies. When you look at these images, your mind is tricked into thinking it is looking at only one scene. It is not difficult to create these matched pairs of slightly different pictures.

## HOW DO HIDDEN DIMENSIONS PICTURES WORK?

If you look closely at any Hidden Dimensions picture, you will see that it contains narrow vertical strips, or columns, about an inch wide, repeated across the image. Each strip looks almost like its neighboring strips— but if you look very closely, you will notice that there are slight differences from column to column.

When you stereoview one of these pictures, your eyes will be looking at different places on the page. Your *left* eye will be looking at one column, and your *right* eye will be looking at the next column to the *right*. When your brain processes what your two eyes are looking at, it will pick up those slight differences between the two columns, interpreting them as depth. Voilà!

The truly amazing thing about Hidden Dimensions pictures is that once you can see the depths, your eyes can wander over a very large image—and your eyes are always looking at two neighboring columns.

# A BRIEF HISTORY OF 3-D

The field of three-dimensional pictures began in 1938, when Sir Charles Wheatstone drew simple diagrams on sheets of paper and viewed them using a large contraption made up of mirrors and sliding panels. He drew two diagrams imitating the slightly different perspectives that our two eyes see when they look at an object. When he peered at these diagrams through his contraption, the mirrors helped him visually fuse the two large drawings, and he saw his diagrams in three full dimensions. In the illustration at right, I've redrawn one of Wheatstone's earliest figures in a size that is easy to stereoview, so that you can see just what he saw. Notice that the two pictures are nearly identical, but there are slight differences between them, as if one is seen slightly from the left and the other slightly from the right.

His discovery made a small stir within the scientific community, but it remained little more than a novelty until several years later, when photography was invented. Early pioneering photographers turned almost immediately to three-dimensional photography as a way to add extra realism to their pictures. If you look at the earliest images from the dawn of the photographic era, such as tintypes,

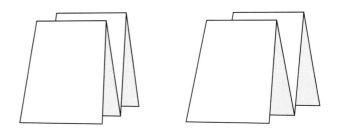

ambrotypes, or daguerreotypes (pictures on tin, glass, or copper), you will find numerous examples of stereoscopic pairs of images. So you might say that photography and stereoscopy grew up side by side.

In the earliest days, when photographic emulsions were not very sensitive and it was necessary to open a camera shutter for as long as a minute for a proper exposure, it was difficult to make stereoscopic pictures. Imagine how difficult it would be to sit still for a full minute and then continue to freeze your pose as the photographer changed film and moved his bulky camera a few inches to take another picture! But eventually, as film speeds improved, and manufacturers designed cameras with two lenses that took two pictures simultaneously, the field of 3-D photography began to grow.

By the 1950s, Sir Charles Brewster had invented a portable device for viewing stereoscopic photographs. An improved model was invented by Oliver Wendell Holmes (who, incidentally, later went on to be a United States Supreme Court justice). The Holmes viewer, with its wider field of view and nearly automatic positioning of the image for easy viewing, was so popular that by the 1870s there was one in nearly every fashionable American and European parlor. By this time, almost all photographers were taking stereoscopic photos; these pictures were often their best-selling items. An industry arose to satisfy the demand for stereoviews depicting famous homes, scenic locations, and public figures. Photographers were sent abroad to photograph the entire world (Palestine was a particularly popular subject), and their work would sell in boxed sets of fifty or one hundred cards. Whenever a natural disaster such as a flood or earthquake occurred, hordes of stereoscopic photographers would descend—much as television crews do today—to photograph the mayhem and destruction. Photographers would also set up studios and shoot pictures depicting humorous events or telling a story through a series of cards. If you were in a public place, you might even find large viewing machines that resembled today's jukeboxes, which would show you a few dozen stereoscopic cards, one by one, all for a penny. Stereoscopic photographs from this era documented every aspect of society, from technology to art to pornography to wars and current events!

Today's collectors of those old photographic cards think of the heyday era as being bracketed by the first two wars that were most extensively photographed in 3-D: the American Civil War and the First World War. By the 1920s, with the rise of cinema, stereoscopy began to wane. The big companies eventually folded, and their priceless stocks of film negatives were gradually consolidated. Today, several million surviving negatives from the American companies are held by the California Museum of Photography at Riverside.

Stereoscopic arts experienced revivals every few years, in such forms as the ViewMaster® reels, and 3-D comic books and films in the 1950s. In the 1950s, anaglyph methods became popular for making 3-D comic books and movies (although the process had been created many decades earlier). Anaglyph methods worked by combining two pictures into one print, one in red ink and the other in green. You would wear glasses that had red over one eye, and green over the other eye. Each eye could see only the picture printed in ink of the opposite color. There was a spate of three-dimensional movies made in the United States starting in 1950, until 1953 when the fad died down as quickly as it had arisen. About the same time, some of the top film directors began making three-dimensional films (Hitchcock's *Dial M for Murder* was filmed in 3-D, but it was never released in that format). Modern full-color 3-D movies can be shown by using special projectors that combine two overlapping images—the glasses we wear make sure that the correct image reaches each of our eyes.

But no matter what method is employed, the basic idea behind 3-D is always the same— to present each eye with a slightly different picture, in which the elements are shifted slightly from side to side. And today, in the form of these Hidden Dimensions images, they are making yet another comeback!

You can find 3-D everywhere, sometimes in places you least expect. For example, geographers commonly study land formations using three-dimensional images that are photographed from airplanes or weather balloons. Sophisticated computer programs analyze photographs taken by satellites to construct surface maps of the earth and the moon. The technique has even been used during wartime by spy planes to calculate the depths of harbors—an airplane might have a film camera mounted on each wing tip to provide two views of everything it flies over. Or a satellite might take two images as it moves across the sky.

Anyone who has taken a course in organic chemistry has probably stumbled across a stereoscopic pair of drawings depicting a large, complex molecule. Such drawings are helpful to chemists, since understanding the shape of a molecule can be crucial for figuring out its interactions.

Three-dimensional studies can be found in every scientific discipline. In medicine, for example, one often finds three-dimensional studies of arteries to help identify problems. The resulting images can be quite dramatic. Ophthalmologists, naturally enough, use 3-D a great deal. Certain eye conditions are best spotted with the use of a special, tiny camera that takes a 3-D photo of the inside back of the eye from two perspectives a few millimeters apart—the pupil is just wide enough so that this stereo picture can be taken from outside the eye!

Three-dimensional viewers are even commonly found in certain government agencies. Faced with the difficult task of spotting forged currency, government technicians often turn to stereoscopic examination of suspicious legal tender. On one side, they put a known legitimate bill, and on the other, the bill they want to test. When they stereoview the two, even the slightest variation in positions will appear to pop off or recede beneath the surface. A forger can engrave plates remarkably close to the original, but it is awfully difficult to match the fraction-of-a-millimeter tolerances that can be identified using this technique!

For those of you who are amateur photographers, it's quite easy to take 3-D photographs yourself. You don't need any fancy equipment. Just one camera is sufficient, as long as you are taking pictures of an object that does not move at all. Try this: Take a picture, move the camera about three inches to the side, and take another picture. That's it! When you develop the prints, place them side by side and look at them through a Holmes viewer, or see if you can stereoview them without the use of any viewer at all.

You can even construct a viewer yourself: Find two magnifying lenses that are about three inches in diameter, and position them so that you are looking through the outer edges of the lenses, as you see in the figure on page 11. If you do it just right, the lenses not only will magnify, but will help refract (bend) the light so that it is easier to stereoview your photographs.

In time, you will refine your photographic abilities. You may notice that using a flash works well only if the flash does not move with the camera. You may also notice that you can augment the depth effect if you shift the camera more than three inches between the two photos; this is called hyperstereo, and I use it if I am photographing a scenic landscape or something that is very distant. How far should I move the camera? There is no exact guide. If I am taking a hyperstereo photo of some distant objects, I usually say to myself, "If I were a giant, looking out at that scene, how far apart would my eyes be, in order for me to see those distant buildings in full depth?" And then I use that guess as the distance between my two cameras.

Serious enthusiasts will buy special equipment, such as a pair of matched cameras and a slide bar to rest them on, or special 3-D cameras of the type that were manufactured in the 1950s. There are even throwaway cameras you can buy today, which take "flicker-type" pictures with some depth effect to them. For more about the wonders of 3-D, write the National Stereoscopic Association at P.O. Box 14801, Columbus, OH 43214. The association's bimonthly publication, *Stereo World*, reports on a surprising wealth of topics—history, calligraphy, Dali, philately, electron microscopy—all in three dimensions.

# MODERN COMPUTER-GENERATED STEREOGRAMS

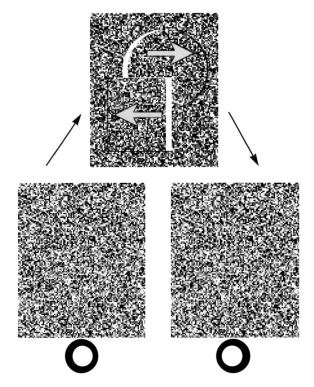

D r. Christopher Tyler was the first to create computer-generated autostereogram images, in 1983. In fact, it was he who coined the general term *autostereogram* to describe them (the prefix *auto-* reflects the images' self-similar nature).

As is the case for any great invention, you can trace the seeds of the idea further back. Dr. Tyler was a researcher studying human vision and depth perception under a noted scientist, Dr. Bela Julesz, who has been using computers to draw 3-D random-dot images for several decades. As early as the 1950s, Dr. Julesz was studying how people perceive depth. But he didn't want to show 3-D photographs to his test subjects, since this might introduce unwanted elements into his experiments involving object recognition, perception of shadows, light and dark, and so forth. Instead, he used a computer to draw pairs of random-dot images that his test subjects would observe through a special viewer. His work was a very early example of computer-generated graphics, and he continues his research using sophisticated equipment that projects these random-dot designs in various ways.

To create these images, Dr. Julesz first generated a square filled with random black or white dots. Then, to build the paired image, he took the first square and shifted a group of dots within it, to the right or left. Where any gap opened up because of this shifting, he simply filled in more random dots. That's all one needs to create a random-dot pair.

Chris Tyler reasoned that there must be some way to eliminate all this duplication, yet retain the 3-D effect. In 1983, he invented a computer-based method for doing this. He published some articles in the scientific literature describing his methods, but it remained little more than a curiosity. A colleague of his, Dr. David Stork, also began producing autostereograms, and published one on the inside cover of a book about light and vision, titled *Seeing the Light* (John Wiley & Sons, 1986).

In 1989, I was a graduate student at the University of California at Berkeley, studying computer graphics, when a friend of mine tossed a photocopy of a random-dot design on my desk and said, "This is supposed to be 3-D, but I can't see it. Can you?"

I had seen Dr. Julesz's random-dot designs, but I had never seen a single image before. "Where's the other half?" I asked.

"There isn't another half. It's just one image."

"That's impossible," I said. "There's got to be another half. In order to see anything 3-D, you need two images. And this thing is so big that even if you found the other half, you'd need a special viewer to see it."

"Well, I don't know how it works, but there are two black marks in it you're supposed to look at."

I had been stereoviewing pictures for nearly two decades; my introduction to three-dimensional images came from a stereoscopic pair of photographs my brother had given me when I was about seven. When I first learned how to look into that pair of NASA photographs, and I saw the Gemini spacecraft floating above the earth, I was

hooked! In the decades that followed, I began collecting the old-fashioned stereoview cards, and gradually improved my eye control so that I can freely view those without a special gadget.

So when my friend insisted that this photocopy had a 3-D effect, it took only a few seconds for me to stereoview the two black marks. To my surprise, I saw an entire image pop off the page, with large block letters saying SEE-ING THE LIGHT.

I was completely surprised. You weren't supposed to be able to see 3-D without two images, but here was one picture that seemed to break all the rules! It was like magic. "Where did you get this?"

"Someone had it, and I photocopied it."

There was no name on the enigmatic image, which looked like a tenth-generation photocopy, so I had nothing to go by. But by that evening, I had figured out how the image had been generated, and I soon began creating my own random-dot images as a hobby.

I immediately began to play with the limitations of the technology. This method worked neatly for making large flat shapes floating off the page, but I found that I could also create the illusion of nicely rounded shapes with a terracing technique. Somehow, our minds were able to piece together the rounded shapes very well, even from remarkably scant information. I've re-created one of my earliest images here—the original version may be found in the May/June 1990 issue of *Stereo World*. It was this magazine article, incidentally, that launched the craze that has mushroomed in popularity all over the world—artists who saw my early images, and read my description of how they were produced, began making their own autostereograms and collaborated

from Chris Tyler's or David Stork's methods. In fact, their methods work better than mine for black-and-white random-dot designs, but don't work well when you try to use them for images that are not composed of simple random dots. My method is used for the sorts of color images you see in this book, and most of the artists who create full-color autostereograms appear to prefer it. Even more remarkable are the numerous variations that crop up here and there, as artists push the limits of the field.

No discussion of autostereograms would be complete without mention of Alfons Schilling and Masayuki Ito, two artists who created autostereogramlike images before Chris Tyler. In 1970, Masayuki Ito created a random-patterned autostereogram, inspired by the work of Bela Julesz. Since the mid-1970s, Alfons Schilling has been creating remarkable hand-drawn art that can be stereoviewed just like any of the images in this book, to produce vivid depth effect. It is all the more surprising that Schilling achieved these precise effects without resorting to a computer's precise drawing abilities. Both these artists created their images using a column-by-column approach that didn't quite achieve the flexibility or generality of the Tyler and Stork methods, but one must consider them autostereograms nevertheless.

with me to produce the earliest commercial items. The phenomenon continues to grow today.

Despite my efforts to find the inventor, it took several years before I found out the source of that first image—imagine my chagrin when I realized that the words *Seeing the Light* were no less than the title of the book that contained it! Also to my surprise, I learned that the method I had created for making these images was slightly different

# KNOT, OR NOT?

Perhaps by now, you've found your mind unraveling a little bit?

Instead, how about trying to mentally unravel the loops in the next few puzzles. When you stereoview each of these pictures, you'll find a twisted, balled-up mass of string. Your goal is to imagine untangling that string and straightening it out as best you can, so that you can answer one question: Is the string a simple loop, or is it knotted?

This puzzle was inspired by a rainy-day game my older brother invented when we were children. He tied a short piece of string into a loop or a knot, and then shaped it into a tangled mess. Then, he laid it down on the table before me.

"Without touching it, can you figure out if it's a knot, or not?"

This was an awfully tough puzzle for a young child like me. I tried to pick out extraneous loops that didn't seem to be looped around any other piece of string, and then I tried to imagine the tangled string with those loops deleted from it. I could usually keep a mental image of one or two loops thus annulled, but by the third, the whole thing would fall apart in my head like a house of cards.

Eventually, I found a way of cheating. I noticed that my brother used the same knotted loop of string for all his "knotted" challenges, and the same unknotted string for his "loop" challenges. So all I had to do was recognize the particular piece of string to know the answer! I would make a big show of peering intently, as if I were thinking hard about the problem, and then I would announce my answer with certainty. My brother was quite impressed. Later, I admitted how I had been arriving at my answers—and he never played that game with me again!

In these puzzles, the only way you can cheat will be to look at the answers in the back of the book. But before you do that, consider the example on the facing page, which shows you the sort of mental gymnastics you should try to do. Try to identify segments of string that encircle empty space, and that don't loop around any other string. Then picture how the tangles would look if these empty loops were eliminated one by one. If you can continue the process to eliminate enough loops, in the end you will be left with either a knot or a simple loop!

18

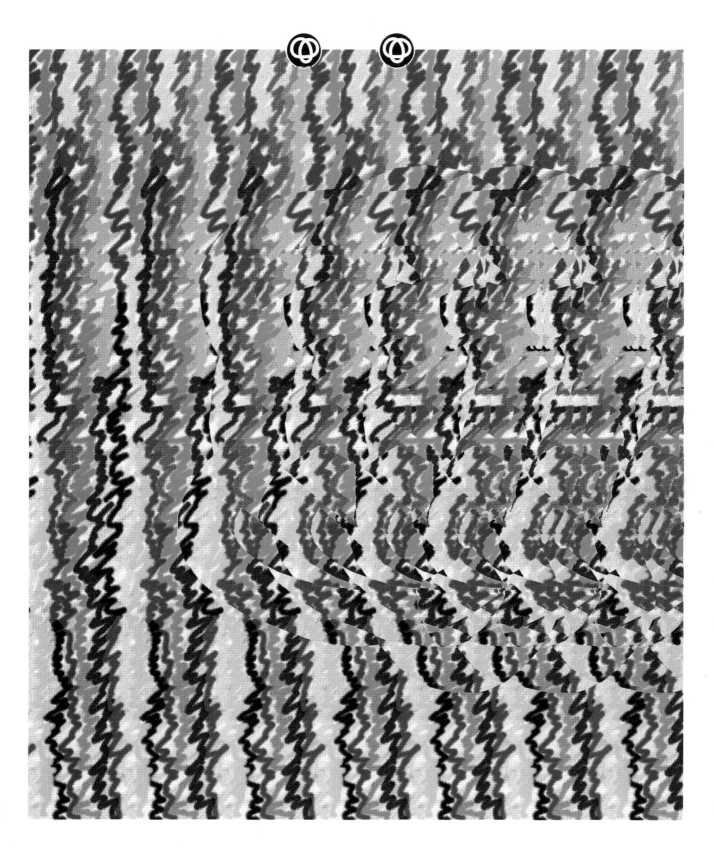

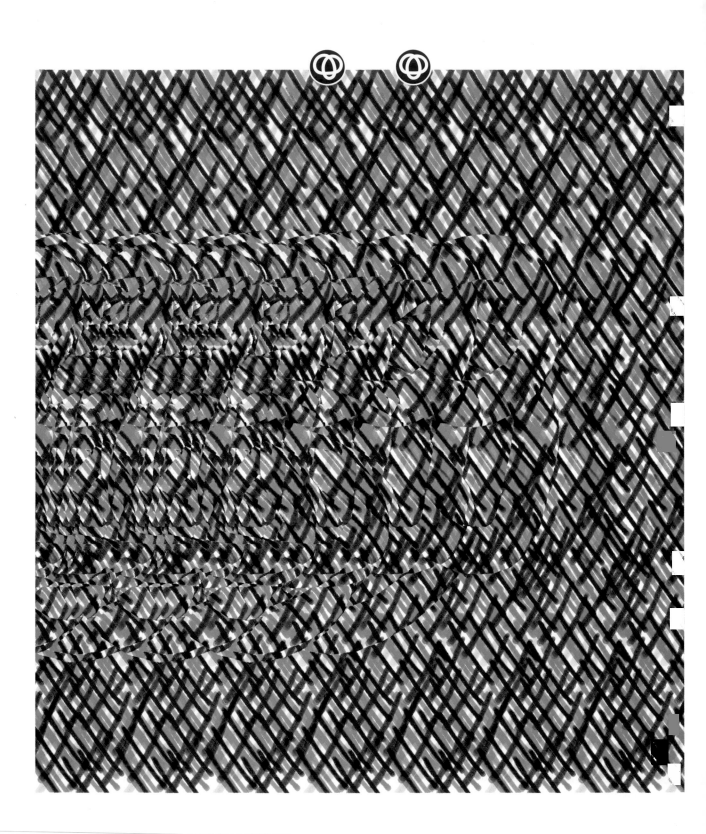

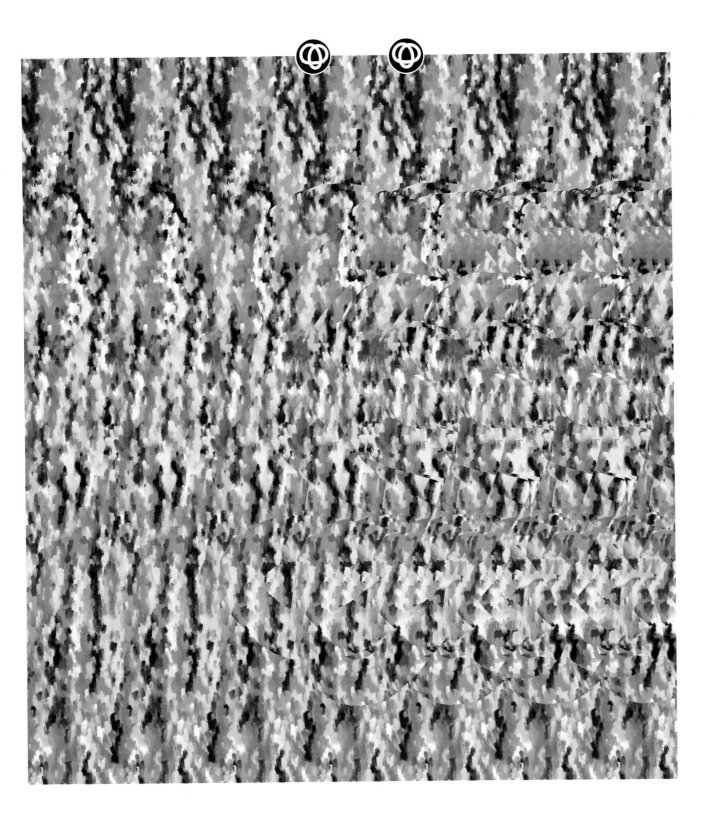

# THE HOPPING MAZE PUZZLES

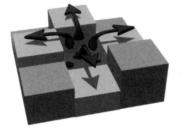 

When you stereoview the image on the opposite page, you will see what looks like a set of stacked blocks. It's actually a maze, though.

The object is to move from the top, where you see a figure jumping onto the board, down to the bottom, where you see another figure preparing to jump off. But there are rules about how you can move from block to block. The rules all deal with how high the blocks are, so this is a puzzle that can be displayed only in three dimensions.

The first rule is that each step you take must move either up or down. You can't move from one block to another block that is the same height.

Second, you are allowed to move orthogonally (that is right, left, up, or down) only if you are jumping up to a taller block.

Third, you are allowed to move diagonally only if you are jumping down to a lower block.

To help you remember the directions, you may notice that the small figure who is jumping onto a block near the top of the puzzle is moving orthogonally, and the figure at the bottom who is hopping off is aiming himself diagonally.

Those are all the rules there are. Now, if you wander over the puzzle, you'll find that there is more than one way to walk through it. Can you find *the shortest path* possible?

23

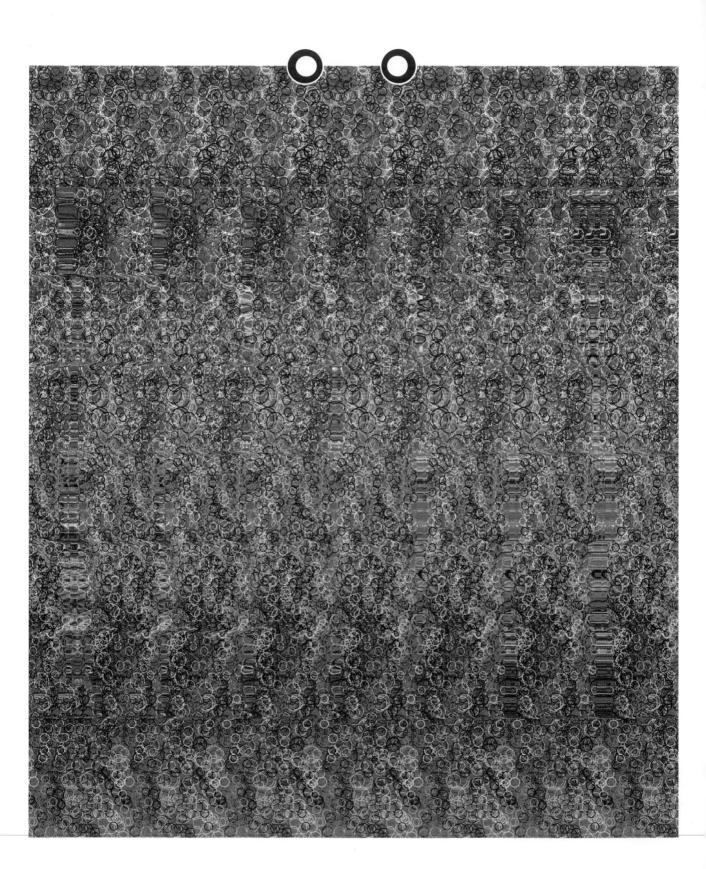

24

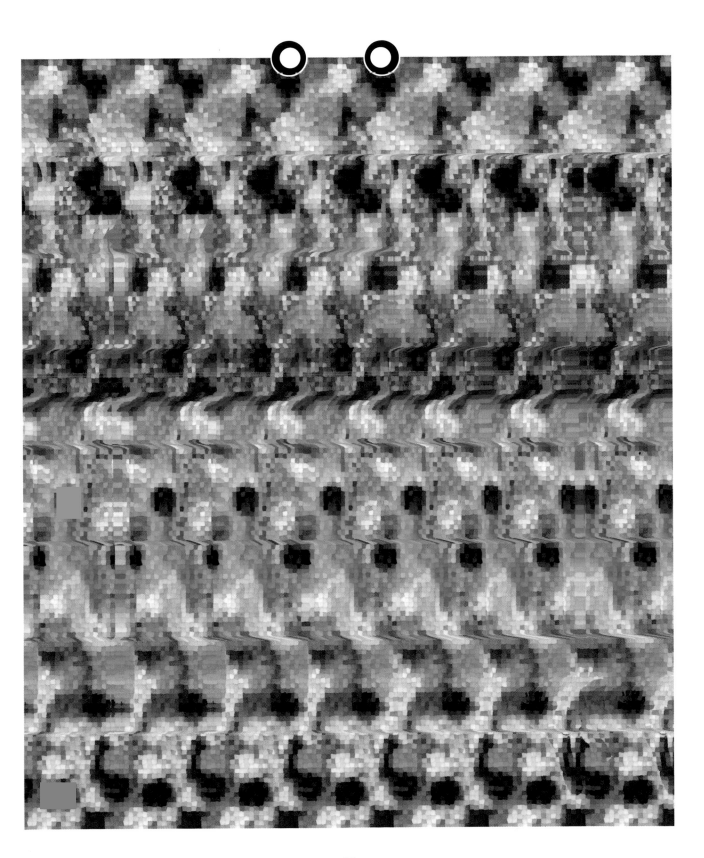

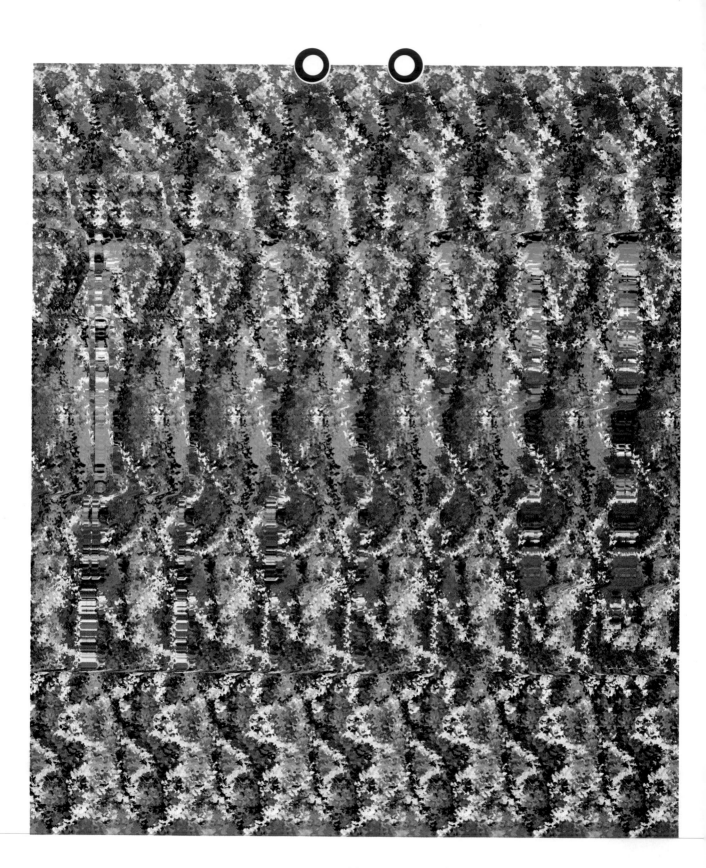

26

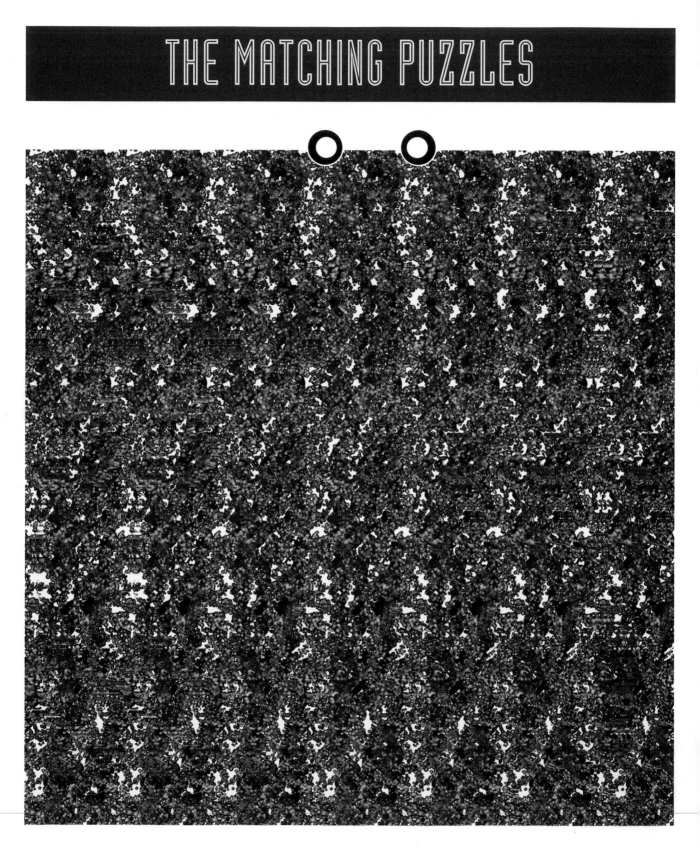

One of these pages contains six tools. The other shows six hands that are holding those tools. Can you match the hands with the tools?

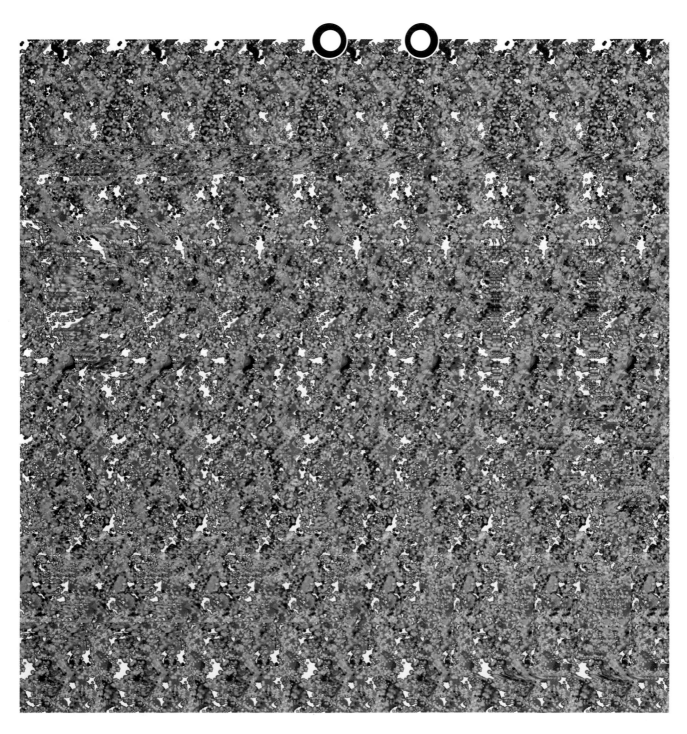

One of these pages contains six musicians. The other shows six instruments.
Can you match the musician with the instrument?

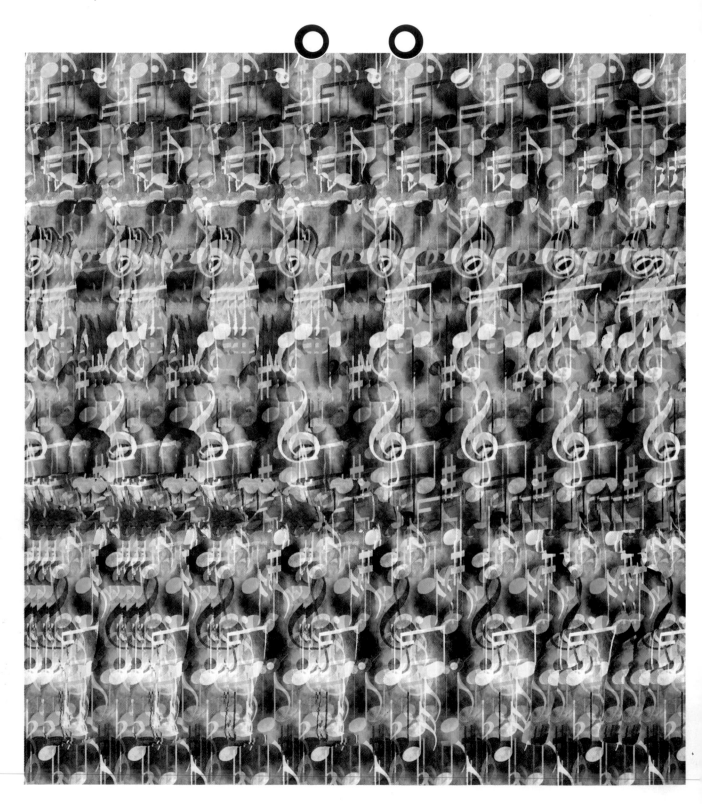

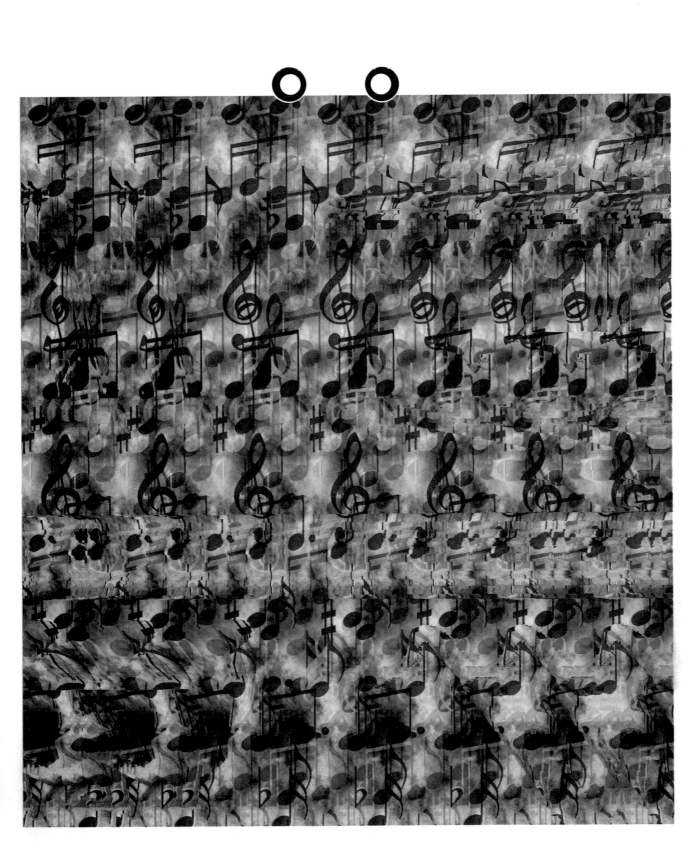

31

# FIND THE MIRROR IMAGES

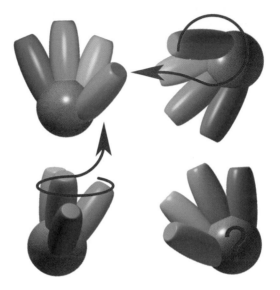

No matter how you position your right hand, you can never get it to look exactly like your left hand. That is because your two hands are mirror images of each other.

I'm sure that if you saw a picture showing several hands, you would be able to pick out which were right hands and which were left hands. Here are some puzzles that ask you to do something similar. You will see several shapes in each puzzle when you stereoview them. Of these shapes, all but one of them will be the same shape, only shown in different perspectives—the one that isn't identical is a mirror image of all the other shapes. Your challenge is to identify which shape is the mirror image.

As an example, the figure above contains four shapes—three of them are identical and

one is the mirror image. I've indicated with arrows how you might rotate two of them so that they will match their neighbor. But the fourth shape, which I've labeled with a question mark, can never be rotated to match any of the other pieces, because it is a mirror image version of them.

Sometimes the most difficult aspect of solving these puzzles is focusing on one identifiable feature that you can use to compare the shapes. In this example, I've colored the lone stick in green so it will stand out as a unique part, and you use it to help you match the shapes to each other. It may help you to pick out some feature that you know must match from shape to shape for each puzzle—and then imagine rotating the pieces so that those features match.

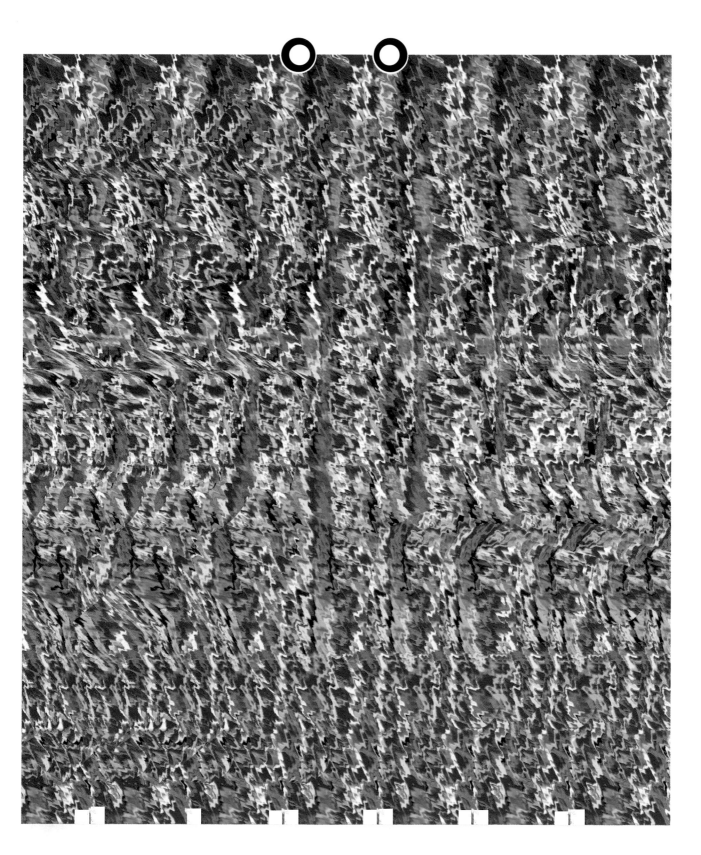

33

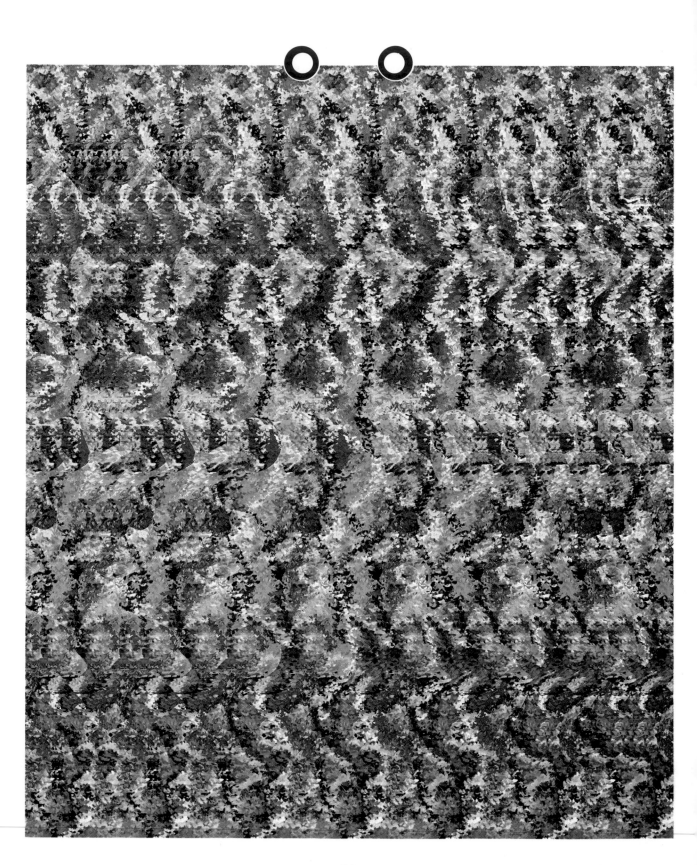

34

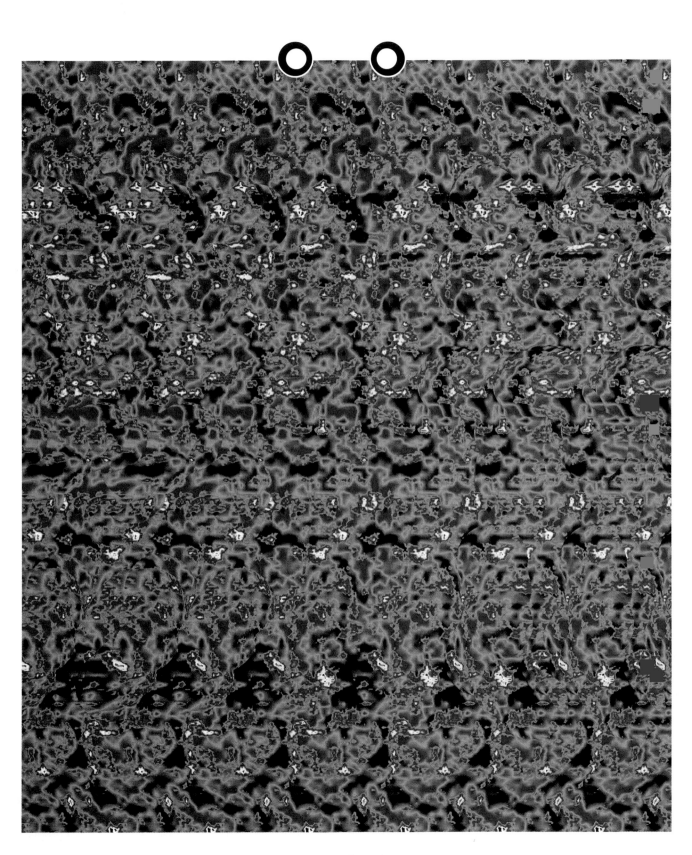

# THE LONG MAZE PUZZLE

The next three pages are all part of a single maze.

You've no doubt seen difficult mazes that have very fine, highly detailed paths you must follow. Such complex mazes can't be easily reproduced as Hidden Dimensions puzzles, because one can't display depths in extraordinarily fine detail. But I've added a wrinkle to this maze—it is spread across several pages.

Start the maze on the facing page, at the top, and follow the pipeline in the same manner you follow an ordinary maze. (Don't think of the pipeline as the walls of the maze. The pipeline is the actual path you must follow.)

If the pipeline crosses over into the next page, then you'll have to turn to the next page and stereoview all over again to start up where you left off.

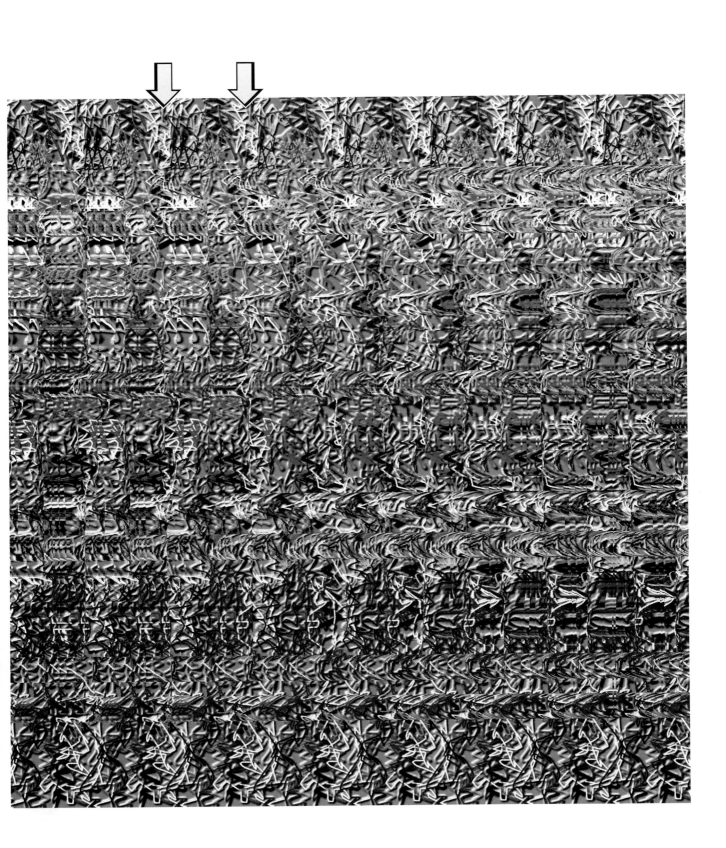

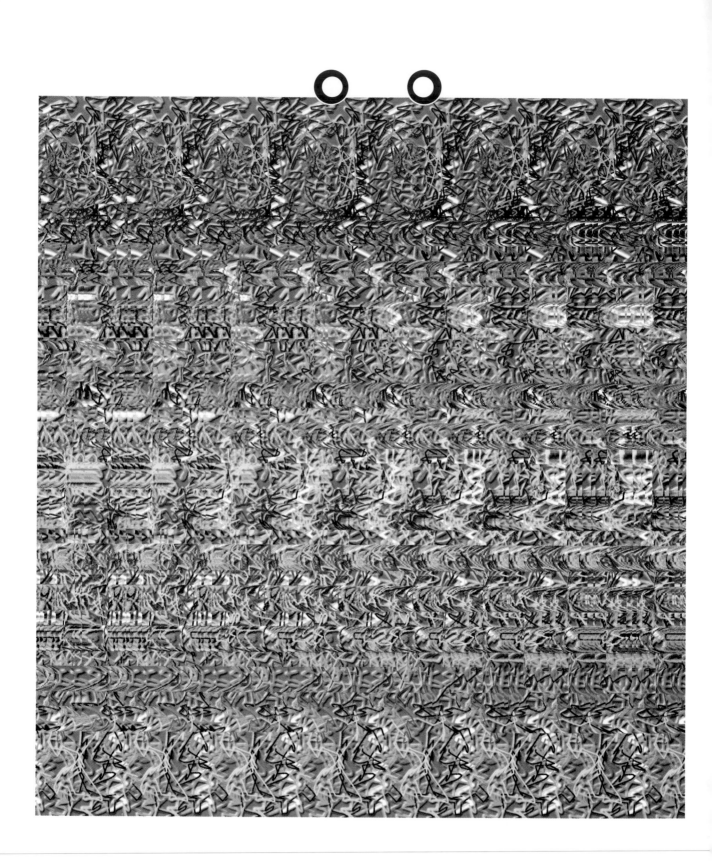

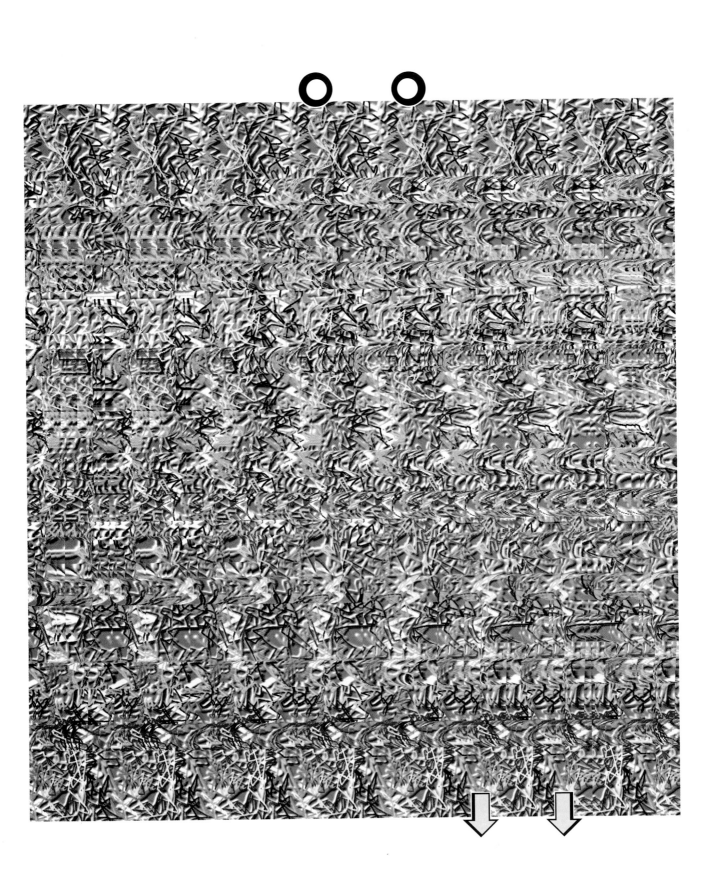

# WHICH TWO PIECES FIT TOGETHER?

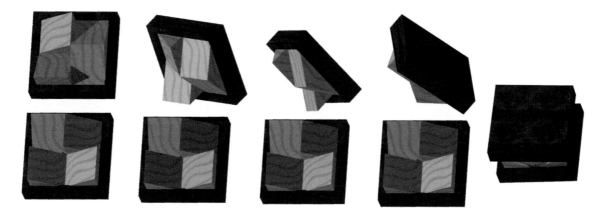

When I was young, I enjoyed playing with a set of toy blocks that snapped together with peglike parts. They were meant for creating architectural models, and that's how I played with them most of the time. But my older brother found a more interesting use for them. He would build small geometric shapes, much like the ones you will see when you stereoview the picture above. Then he would issue me a challenge: "Two of these shapes fit together. Can you tell which ones?"

It wasn't an easy question to answer. I could, of course, pick up the objects and try to fit them together, but I wasn't supposed to do that. Instead, I had to scrutinize them and, in my mind's eye, pick them up, rotate them every which way, and see which two inter-locked perfectly. Then, when I finally decided which two were the correct pair and how they meshed, I would give him my final answer.

Years later, when I found myself building puzzles for this book, I found that my brother's idea translates well into three dimensions. On the next five pages, you will find five puzzles, each portraying a set of similarly shaped blocks. Within each puzzle, two of the blocks are capable of fitting together, like a cast and mold. Your challenge is to figure out which two fit together.

It's not as easy as it sounds. You'll have to mentally pick up a piece and flip it over, then rotate it to see if it fits any of the other pieces. The mental gymnastics of flipping and rotating are particularly difficult to do!

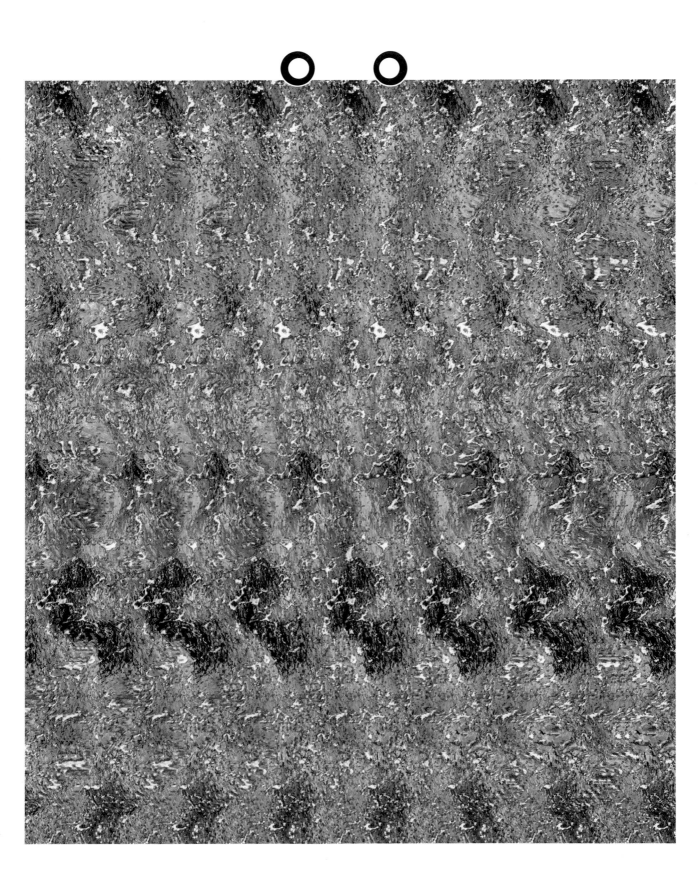

41

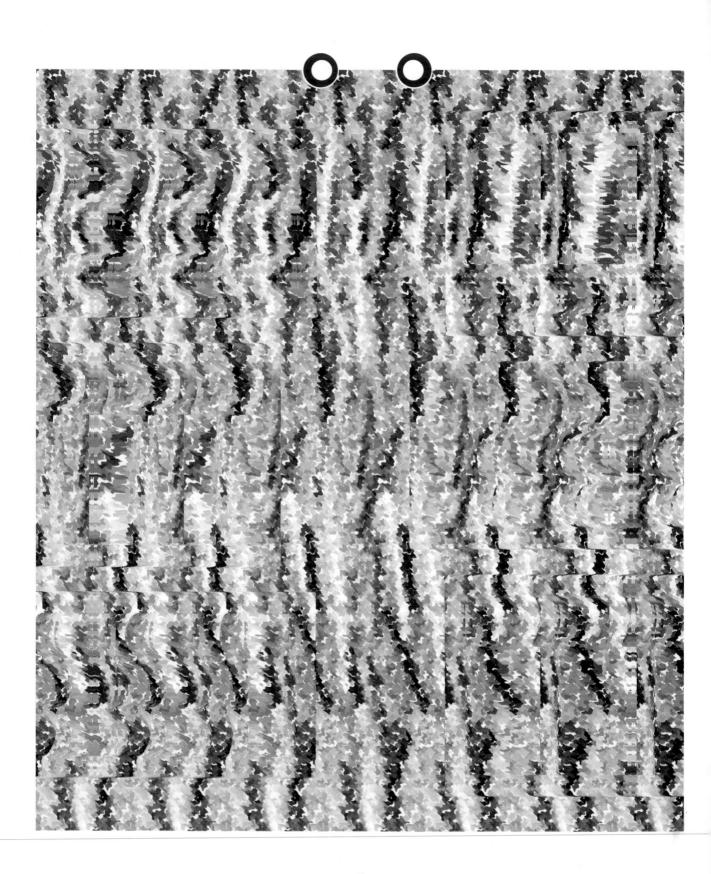

42

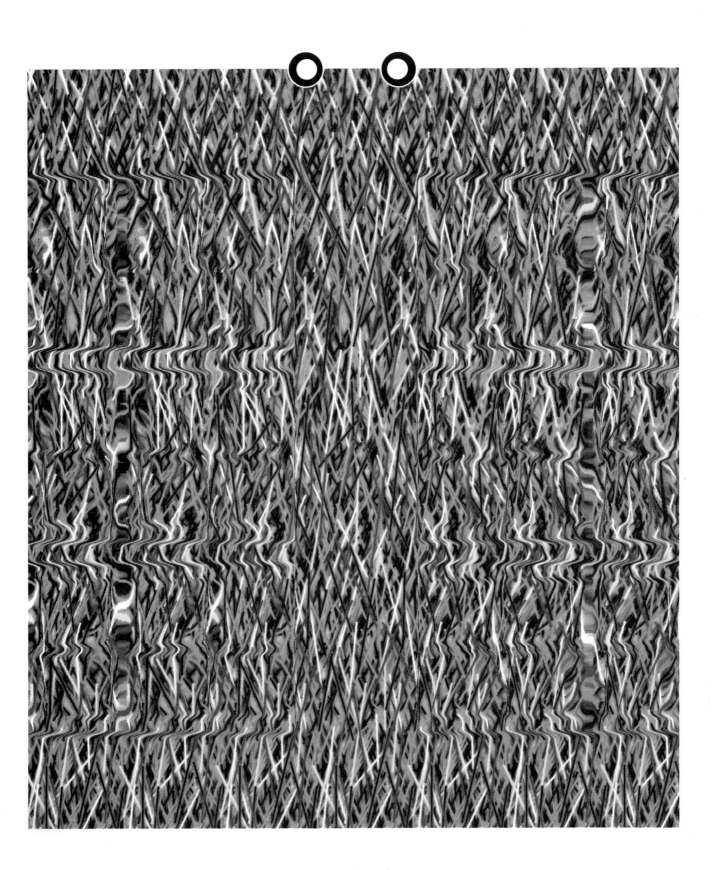

43

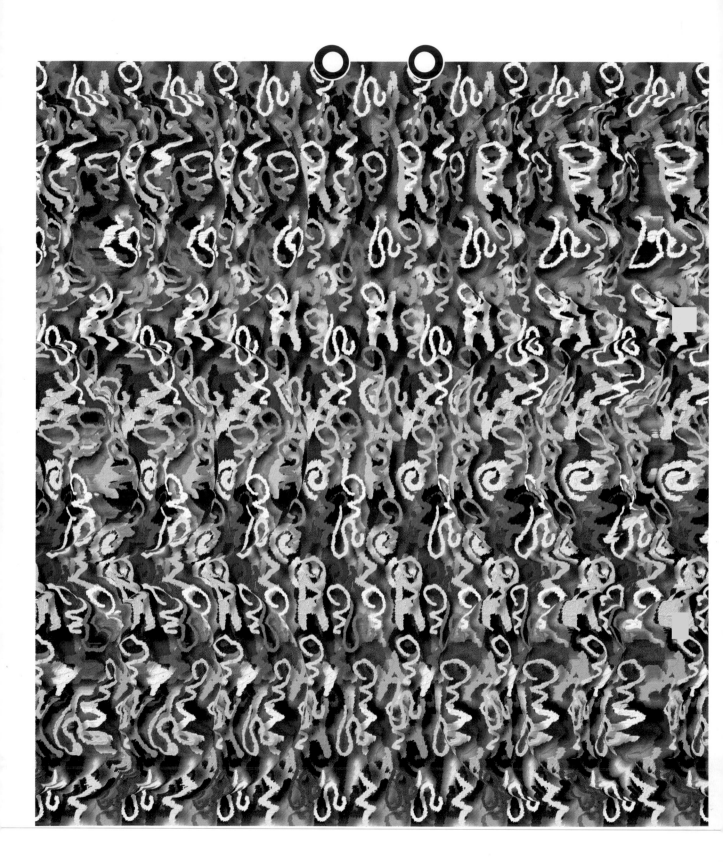

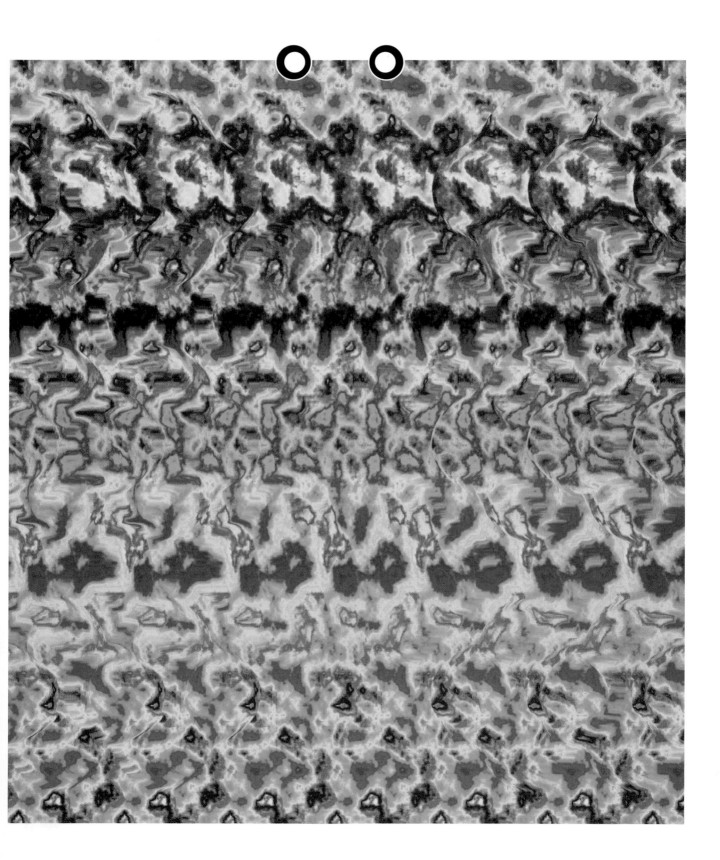

45

# THE AROUND THE GLOBE PUZZLE

The next several pages of the book combine to make more than one puzzle. Your first challenge comes from images below and to the right. When you stereoview these two images, you will see several flat shapes. Each of these is actually the outline of a country. Can you identify them all?

I've made the task a little bit harder by rotating the maps, so instead of the way they usually appear, they might be sideways or upside down. And I've enlarged some, and reduced others, so that you can't identify them by their relative size.

Then, on the six pages following these maps, you will see some famous buildings and landmarks from around the world. Can you match each image to one of the countries whose map I've drawn here?

The last part of the challenge will be the trickiest. When I assembled this book, I placed the scenes of famous buildings in a very specific order. Can you figure out what that order is? Perhaps it has something to do with the maps on these two pages—or with the countries or the buildings themselves—or perhaps not!

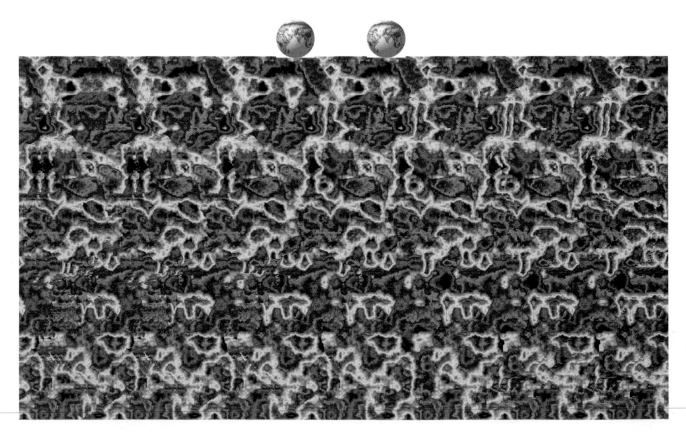

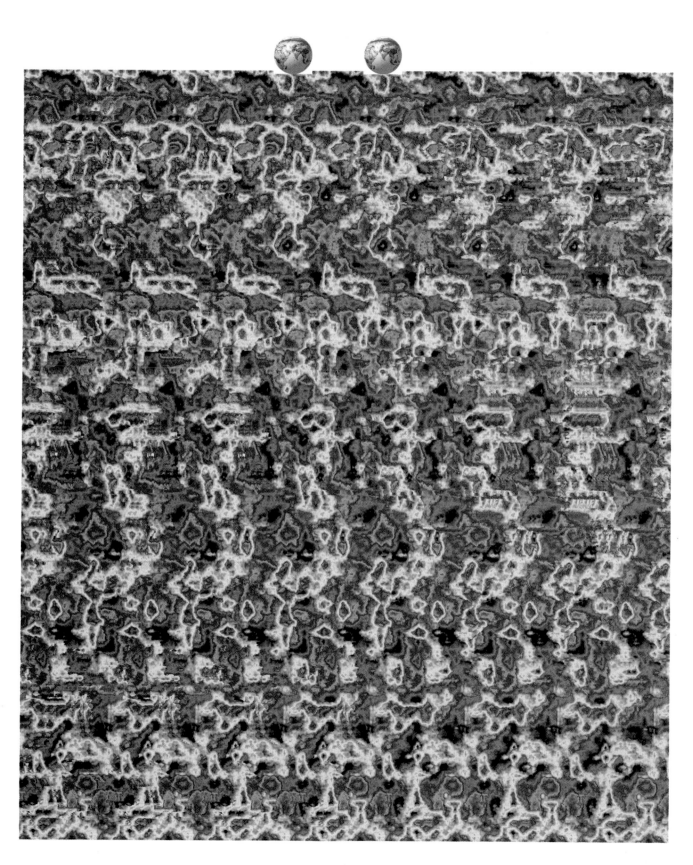

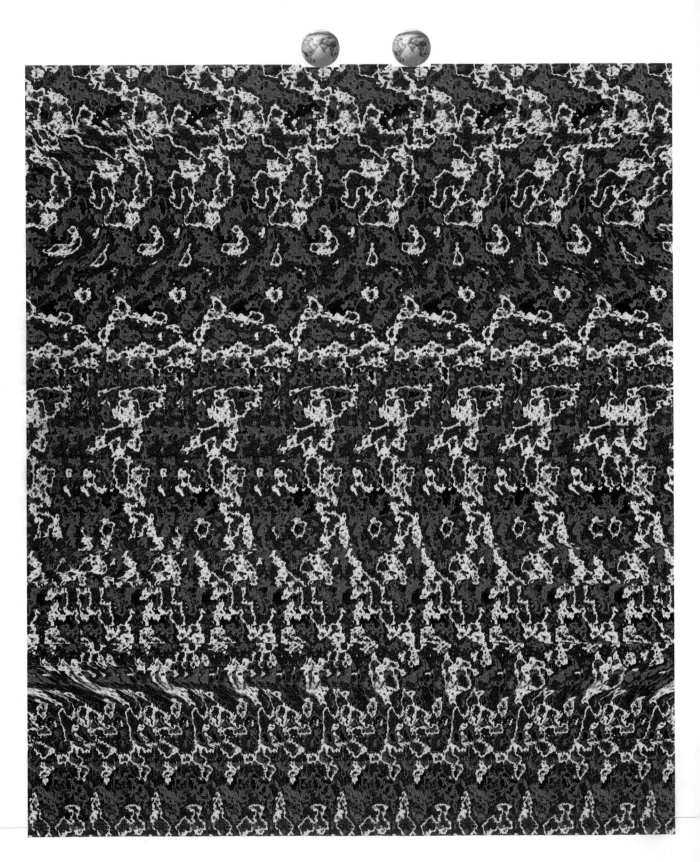

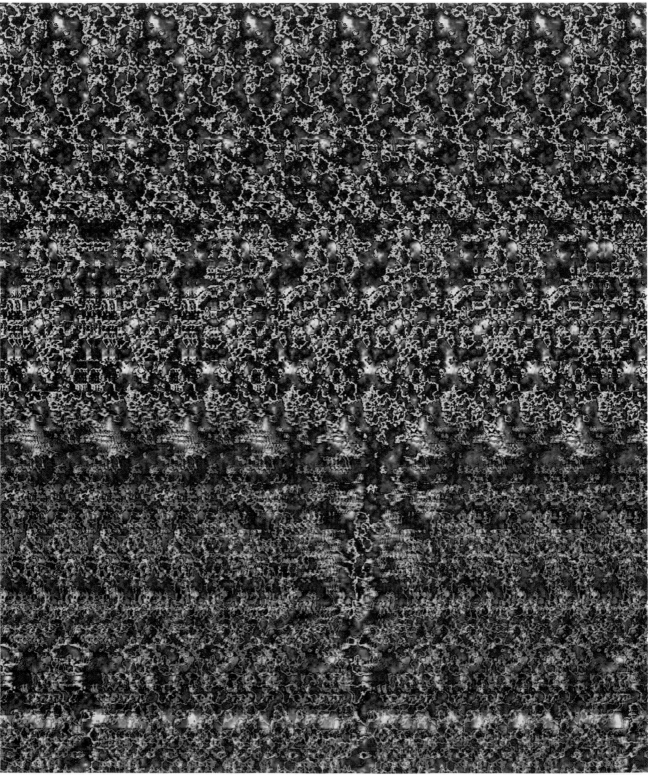

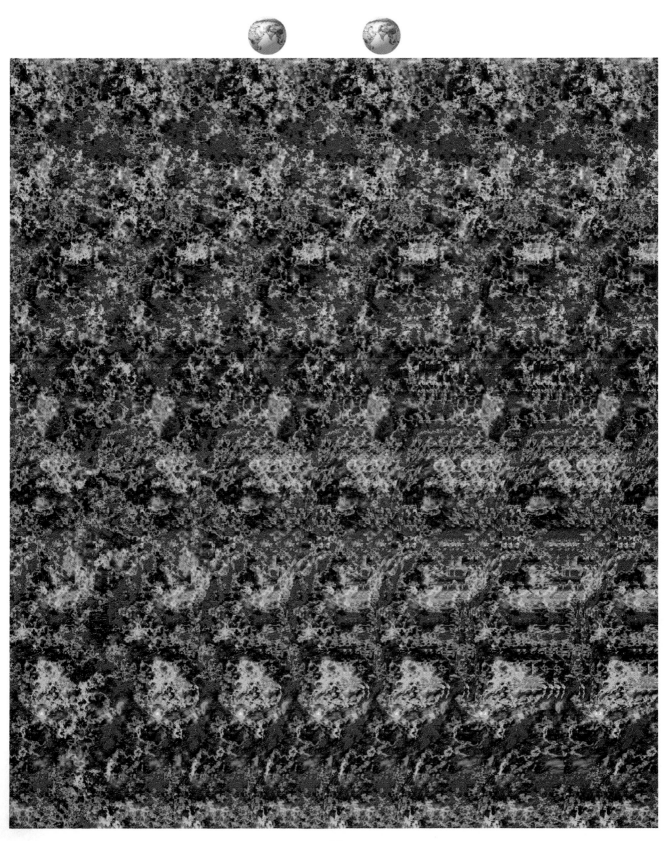

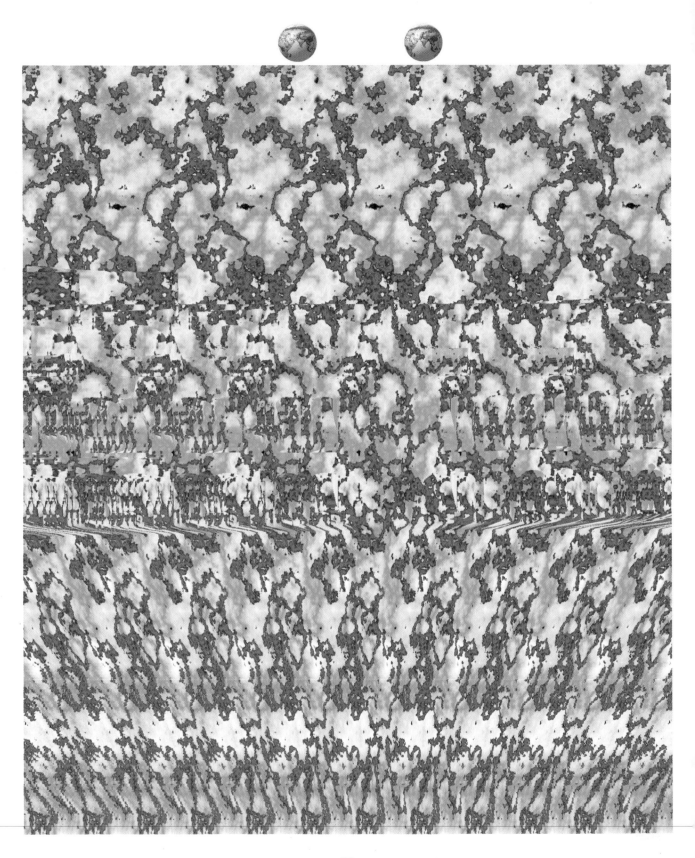

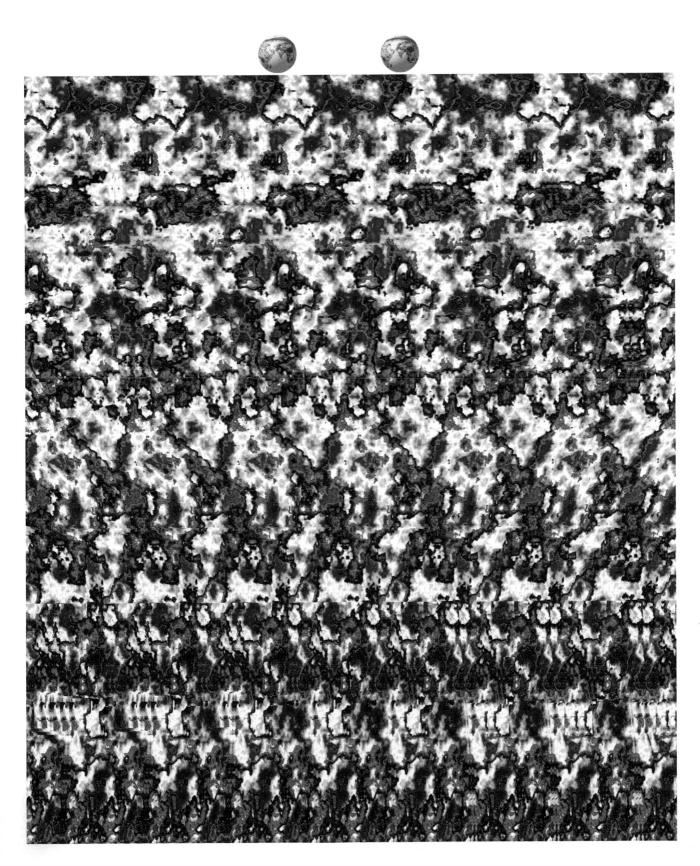

# SOLUTIONS

## Knot, or Not?

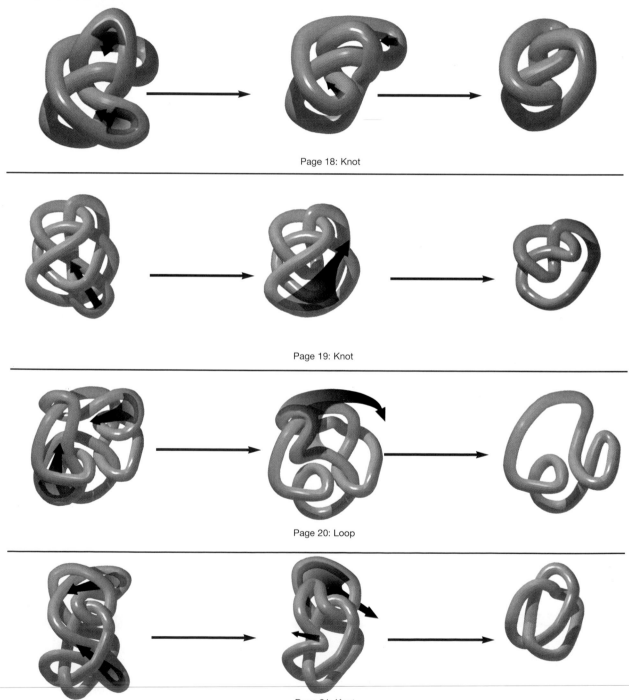

Page 18: Knot

Page 19: Knot

Page 20: Loop

Page 21: Knot

## The Hopping Maze Puzzles

The numbers and shades of gray represent the heights of the squares, where one is lowest and darkest. The arrows show the shortest path from start to finish.

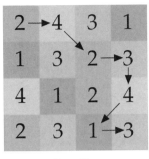

Page 23

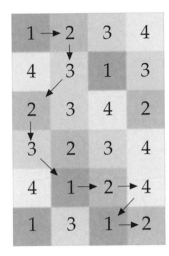

Page 24

Page 25

Page 27

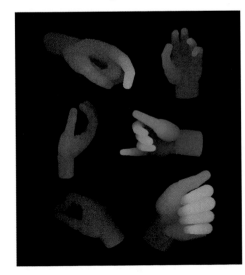

Page 26

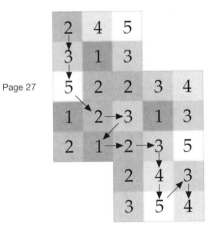

## The Matching Puzzles

Hand using calculator (red)

Hand holding baseball (blue)

Hand holding scissors (green)

Hand holding mug (light green)

Hand holding pen (purple)

Hand throwing dart (gray)

← Page 28          Page 29 →

55

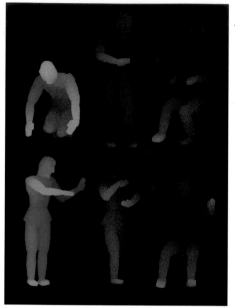

← Page 30

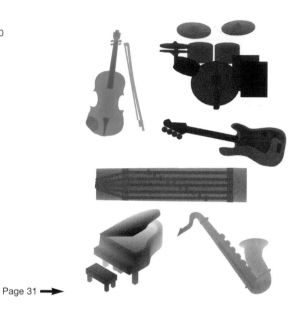

Page 31 →

Musician playing koto (brown)
Musician playing electric guitar (purple)
Musician playing piano (blue)

Musician playing drums (red)
Musician playing saxophone (gray)
Musician playing violin (green)

## Find the Mirror Images

Page 33

Page 34

Page 35

The mirror images are shown here in red, and the matching parts of these shapes are color coordinated.

# The Long Maze Puzzle

Page 37

Page 38

Page 39

# Which Two Pieces Fit Together?

Page 41

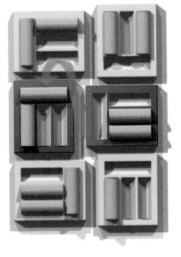

Page 42

Page 43

Page 44

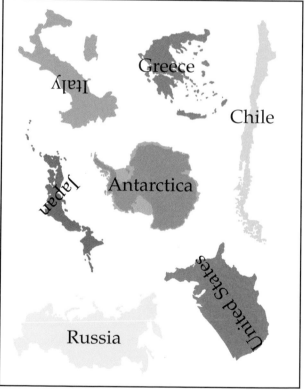

Page 45

## The Around the Globe Puzzle

Page 46 In this group of countries, you should have identified China, France, and India as the locations of the Great Wall of China, the Eiffel Tower, and the Taj Mahal.

What is the order of these buildings?

You might have looked for some clue to the order of the puzzles by considering how the country maps were positioned on the page or how they were rotated—but the buildings are actually arranged according to the age of the buildings, from youngest to oldest.

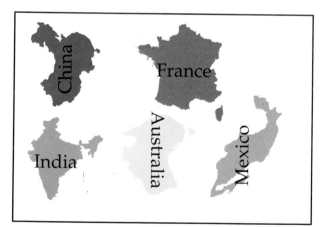

Page 47 In this group of countries, you should have identified Italy, Russia, and the United States as the locations of the Colosseum, the Cathedral of St. Basil, and the Guggenheim Museum.

58

Page 48

The Guggenheim Museum in New York City, U.S.A., was designed by Frank Lloyd Wright in the **1950s**. Its spiral structure, based on the shape of snail shells, makes for a unique museum experience; visitors take the elevator to the top of the dome and walk down the gradually sloped ramp, viewing paintings and sculpture as they slowly descend all the way to the ground floor.

Page 49

The Eiffel Tower in Paris, France, was designed by Alexandre Gustave Eiffel for the Paris Exposition of **1889** and was originally planned as a temporary structure. At 300 meters (984 feet) it was the tallest building in the world in its time. Its curved beams anticipated the current engineering techniques used to build modern skyscrapers.

Page 50

The Taj Mahal in Agra, India, was built by Shah Jahan as a mausoleum for his beloved consort, who was endearingly called Taj Mahal, or Crown of the Palace. The 57-meter-high structure completed in **1648** represents the pinnacle of Mogul architecture. One of the most breathtaking features of this building is its pure white marble surface that stands out among the reddish buildings that surround it.

Page 51

The Cathedral of Saint Basil in Moscow, Russia, is located just outside the Kremlin and was built in **1560** during the reign of Ivan the Terrible. The exuberant style of architecture, including characteristic brightly painted onion-domes, was derived from wooden buildings styles in Northern Russia. The building, with a central sanctuary surrounded by eight chapels, is the symbol of the Russian Orthodox church.

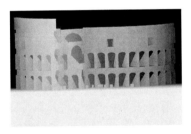

Page 52

The Colosseum in Rome, Italy, was built in the years **69 to 80** by the Roman emperors Vespasian and Titus. Seating 50,000 spectators, the arena was used for gladiator fights and macabre animal versus human spectacles, and the floor could even be flooded for mock naval battles. During the Middle Ages, much of the 150-foot-high outer structure was quarried to build other buildings in Rome.

Page 53

The Great Wall of China was built in the **third-century B.C.** by Shi Huangdi of the Ch'in dynasty to protect the northern frontier regions from invasion. In the event of attack, soldiers could race along its top, from turret to turret, 15 meters above the enemy. Gates positioned at intervals along its 1,500-mile length permitted trade with the outside world. Ironically, the more recent Ming dynasty, which had renovated many of these gates, was toppled by invaders who secretly slipped past the fortified wall through those very gates.

# APPENDIX: JUST FOR FUN

I've cooked up a smattering of enticing images in my labora-
tory to show you some interesting aspects of autostereograms. These aren't puzzles, but you may find them puz-
zling nevertheless!

## HOW DEEP IS DEEP?

See how far you can follow the two slopes—one coming off the page, one
going in. Notice how difficult it is to follow these ramps from the left all the
way to the right.

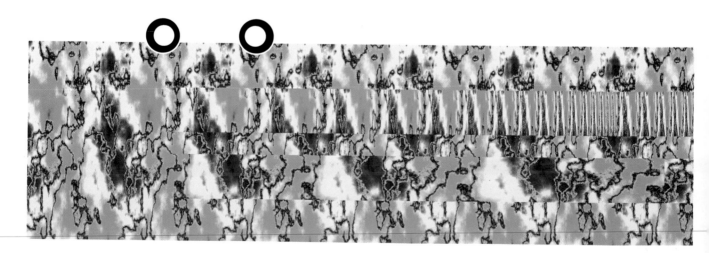

## AMBIGUITY

If you stereoview this image and follow the contour of the elevated ring, you will notice an extra crescentlike arc toward the right half of the ring. But when you look at the triangle, that arc disappears.

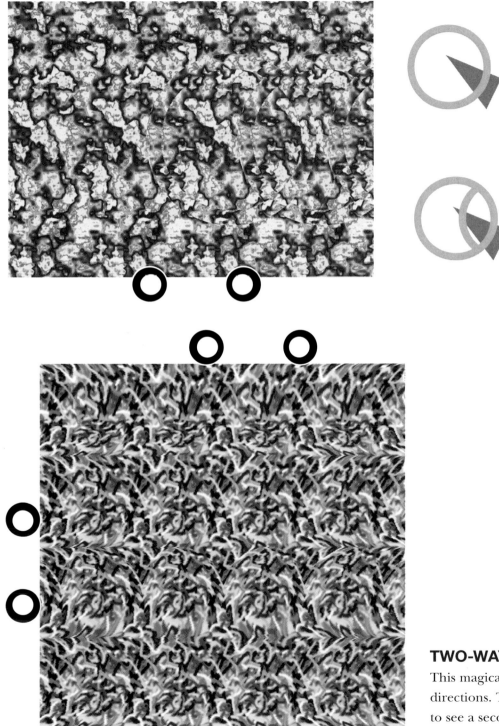

## TWO-WAY DEPTHS

This magical picture works in two directions. Turn the book on its side to see a second depth design.

61

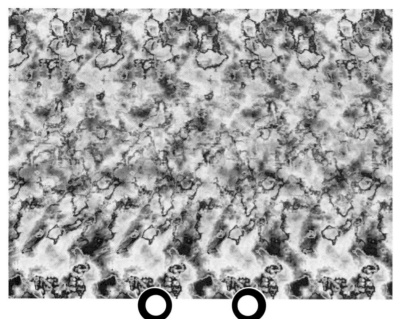

## VAPORIZING SPHERE

This ethereal sphere gradually becomes transparent at its top.

## A COLORED TEAPOT

It's tricky to add specific colors to particular locations in a Hidden Dimensions picture, but it's possible. Can you see the design I've faintly colored onto the teapot?

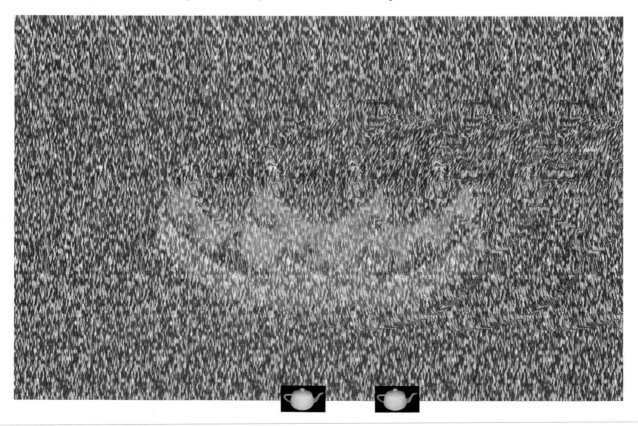

# CLOSING NOTES

I hope you enjoyed this excursion through Hidden Dimensions pictures. Now that you've learned to stereoview, try it out on the world around you. There are hidden depths to be found everywhere you look! Try stereoviewing the patterns in a floor . . . a sculpted molding of a building . . . Who knows what you'll find?

The most creative discovery of an unintended three-dimensional photograph that I've ever heard about was by a baseball aficionado who noticed that a line of photographers were all snapping pictures as a baseball player slid into home plate. He gathered their photos together and found two that happened to have been taken at exactly the same instant. And because they were taken from two nearby vantage points, they made an unintended stereo pair!

It can also be a great deal of fun to draw small pictures by hand and stereoview them. Or you can try drawing pictures on a computer. The best software programs for this purpose are the ones that let you draw individual graphic elements that you can later move around, rather than "painting" programs that apply the graphics permanently onto your image. Create a drawing, duplicate the objects, and then tweak the duplicate copy by moving elements to the left or right a little bit. In a few minutes, you can create your own stereoscopic drawings!

All images in this book were created on an Apple® Macintosh® IIci computer with a DayStar™ accelerator. All modeling, rendering, and composing software used to create the Hidden Dimensions images was written by the author. Most of the photorealistic illustrations and diagrams were modeled and rendered using RayDream Designer© for the Macintosh. All the random-dot textures and most of the multicolor textures were created using software written by the author. Some multicolor textures were created using Fractal Design Painter™ and Paint Alchemy™ software for the Macintosh computer.

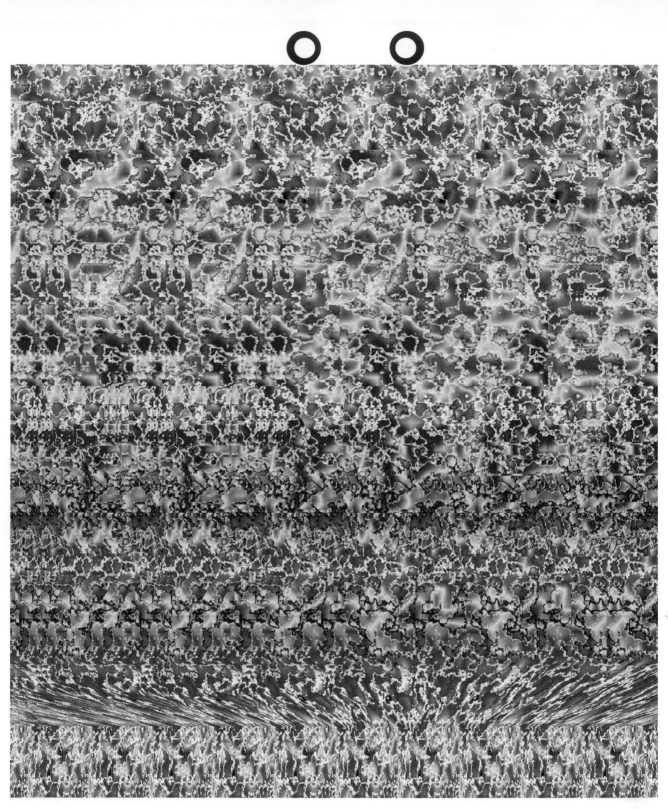

**THE AUTHOR AT WORK**
With his faithful Macintosh, and a cup of tea.